MW01255067

THE KINGDOM DRIVEN

ENTREPRENEUR'S GUIDE TO

GOAL SETTING

*A Kingdom Approach for Setting
and Pursuing Goals to Position You
for God's Best in Business*

SECOND EDITION

SHAE BYNES

The Kingdom Driven Entrepreneur's Guide to Goal Setting: Second Edition

Published by Kingdom Driven Publishing

4846 N. University Drive #406 | Lauderhill, FL, 33351 USA

KingdomDrivenEntrepreneur.com

Published in the United States of America

ISBN: 978-0-9996763-3-2

TABLE OF CONTENTS

`

WHAT'S NEW IN THIS SECOND EDITION?

In 2013, I co-authored the first edition of *The Kingdom Driven Entrepreneur's Guide to Goal Setting* with Antonina Geer (Co-Founder of Kingdom Driven Entrepreneur) based on the first teaching workshops we had ever hosted for the community. I vividly remember when the Holy Spirit spoke to my heart "No more S.M.A.R.T. goals" in order to bring correction to my thinking around setting and pursuing goals in Kingdom business. The Kingdom Driven framework was birthed from those early conversations I had with the Lord.

What's interesting is that at the time of those conversations with the Lord, I still did not have a revelation of doing business by the infinite power of God's grace. For this reason, anyone who read my book *Grace Over Grind: How Grace Will Take Your Business*

Where Grinding Can't prior to reading the first edition of the goal setting guide likely found some of the messaging, despite being Kingdom driven in its approach, to be incongruent.

After walking out this adventure called Kingdom driven entrepreneurship for several years now, I was compelled to create this second edition to capture the revelations, wisdom, and experiences of the past seven years since the first edition was published. So here it is! I'm grateful that you have purchased this guide and pray that you are extraordinarily blessed (empowered to prosper) by the words written within it.

With love,
Shae Bynes
Your Chief Fire Igniter

1

GOAL SETTING AS A GODLY PURSUIT

> *"But seek first the kingdom of God and his righteousness, and all these things will be added to you." Matthew 6:33*

This is a Kingdom Driven Entrepreneur's guide to goal setting, so it is important to begin by defining what a Kingdom Driven Entrepreneur is in the first place.

Kingdom (of God): God's rule and reign, the King's way of being and doing things, the realm of heaven, and the government of God

Driven: Propelled or motivated by

Entrepreneur: One who organizes and operates a

business (or businesses), identifying a need, pain point, or desire and meeting it in the marketplace

When you are a Kingdom Driven Entrepreneur, it essentially means that your entrepreneurial endeavors are *motivated* by seeing an increase of the Kingdom of God on Earth, and are *propelled forward* by first seeking the Kingdom of God and His righteousness knowing that all things will be added unto you. God's priority is to extend His Kingdom on the earth, and as a Kingdom Driven Entrepreneur, you are a co-laborer with God to bring the invisible realities of Heaven to the visible realities of your spheres of influence on earth. It is for this reason that in Matthew 6:10, Jesus Christ instructed us to pray: "Thy Kingdom come, thy will be done on earth as it is in Heaven." As a Kingdom Driven Entrepreneur, your sphere of influence includes the people you encounter through your business endeavors, specific communities, or even industries. Not only do you get to express the good news of the sovereign King Jesus and His Kingdom, drawing people into an encounter and right relationship with God (through word and/or actions); you also have the opportunity to influence and impact situations, systems, and cultures in business with the glorious ways of the Kingdom of God.

What does it mean to seek first the Kingdom of God and his righteousness? It simply means to first pursue

God's ways of being and doing and be aligned with His authority in your life. In *The Message Bible*, Eugene Peterson described it like this: Steep your life in God-reality, God-initiative, God-provisions. Re-read this paragraph and replace each instance of the word *life* with the word *business*.

The fact of the matter is that is not business as usual; it is not the way business operates in the world. When you are a Kingdom Driven Entrepreneur, your business is fully yielded to God (the Ultimate Chief "Any and Everything" Officer) and guided by the Holy Spirit. You allow Jesus Christ to be the Lord of your entrepreneurial journey by prioritizing the King's agenda before anything else. You align your dreams with God's dream for your business by delighting yourself in Him. You seek His heart for the people you serve and the solutions you bring to the marketplace. While some are driven by profits, accolades, power, passion, or freedom and flexibility, a Kingdom Driven Entrepreneur is driven by the Kingdom of God and led by the Spirit of God. In fact, this blesses you with an advantage!

Should we set and pursue goals in business in light of Matthew 6:33?

I believe the answer is yes, albeit in a Kingdom driven manner. A goal is an idea of the future or a desired end result toward which effort is directed. Let's look at a few scripture verses that provide biblical support for the idea of setting goals (Note: bold emphasis is mine).

> *Proverbs 21:5: **The plans of the diligent** lead surely to abundance, but everyone who is hasty comes only to poverty.*

> *Proverbs 29:18: **Where there is no prophetic vision**, the people cast off restraint, but blessed is he who keeps the law.*

> *Habakkuk 2:2: And the Lord answered me: "**Write the vision; make it plain on tablets**, so he may run who reads it.*

> *Philippians 3:13-14: Brothers, I do not consider that I have made it my own. But one thing I do: forgetting what lies behind and straining forward to what lies ahead, **I press on toward the goal** for the prize of the upward call of God in Christ Jesus.*

The objective of this book is to equip you with a Kingdom Driven framework and approach for both setting and pursuing goals for your business. Before getting started though, I want to encourage anyone who feels stressed and anxious about creating business goals (or even thinking about creating them). If this is you, I want you to take a long, deep breath. You are not under *any* pressure to perform or do this perfectly. Consider this to be a fun, enjoyable activity. I always say that doing business in partnership with God is a wild, crazy, and amazing adventure. In this adventure, there will become unknowns, you will be stretched, and it will require taking some risks, but know that you are not alone. The presence of God is always with you. The mighty favor of God surrounds you. The love of God covers you, and the grace of God empowers you to do all you are called to do and to be all you are called to be. Again, you are not under any pressure to perform or do this perfectly. Invite the Holy Spirit into the process and simply thank Him for being your comforter, leading and guiding you into all truth.

If you have already enthusiastically created goals for your business for the quarter or year, I challenge you to revisit them after you have read this book in its entirety, as I believe you'll view and consider your goals from a different lens. Setting and pursuing goals with God, the Ultimate CEO, will help you experience His very best and have a greater Kingdom impact through the work that you do!

2

RE-THINKING S.M.A.R.T. GOALS

> "Do not conform to the pattern of this world, but be transformed by the renewing of your mind. Then you will be able to test and approve what God's will is—his good, pleasing and perfect will."
> Romans 12:2

If you've spent any significant amount of time studying effective goal setting or have worked in a corporate environment, you're likely to have come across a very popular goal setting strategy referred to as S.M.A.R.T. goals. George T. Doran is credited as the originator of this framework from his published work entitled *There's a S.M.A.R.T. way to write management's goals and objectives* in the November 1981 issue of *Management Review*. In his work, he advises that objectives should be: Specific, Measurable, Assignable, Realistic, and

Time-Related. Since the release of his work, the acronym has been interpreted by management consulting industry experts in a variety of ways. For example, the A has been interpreted as "Achievable" or "Acceptable," the R as "Relevant," and the T as "Timely" or "Time-bound." Let's first review the classic model (with some of the alternate interpretations) in greater detail:

Specific

Be clear about what you're seeking to achieve. A specific goal is well defined and has a much greater chance of being accomplished than a vague goal, given that it positions you for identifying the steps needed along the way. For example, "I want to create an exceptional customer experience that yields increased retention rates and referrals."

Measurable

Use concrete "countable" criteria (e.g. "how much", "how many") that can be tracked and measured to determine the progress toward the goal.

Assignable

Specify who will do it. It must be able to be assigned to someone to achieve it, whether it by yourself, a team member, or collectively by your entire team.

Acceptable

Ensure there is a base of support within the organization (stakeholders) to embrace the objective being set.

Achievable (or Realistic)

Create an objective that can be accomplished -- one that stretches you, but is not overly ambitious and unrealistic based on current constraints or resources. It's a goal that you are both willing and able to work toward.

Relevant

Align the goals with your core values and ensure that they contribute toward your broader business goals.

Time-Related (or Time-bound)

Attach a time frame for the accomplishment of the goal in order to give it the proper priority.

The Problem with S.M.A.R.T. Goals

While there is validity in the S.M.A.R.T. model, it simply doesn't provide enough of a solid framework for Kingdom Driven Entrepreneurs who have given Jesus Christ lordship over their businesses and are both led and empowered by the Holy Spirit. Part of the problem lies within these two words: *achievable and realistic.* Framing your goals on a model of achievable and realistic keeps you focused on what you can do in *your own strength.* Focused on what you think is *possible for you to do*. Focused on what you think is *reasonable* and within the constraints of *your current resources*.

You will often hear personal development experts (both Christian and non-Christian) telling you that setting achievable and realistic goals is fundamental to your success in both life and business. They will tell you that by setting unrealistic goals, you are setting yourself up for disappointment and failure. You won't be able to persist when the times get hard because the goal will be so far out of reach. Inevitably, you'll give up, cave in, and quit. These things *can* be true and the reason it is popular advice is because it is indeed practical advice. That said, I want to encourage you to be a bit peculiar in this area because the S.M.A.R.T. framework is the model of the world and leaves out the guidance and wisdom of Almighty God.

A Kingdom Driven Framework

Let's now explore a Kingdom driven approach and framework for goal setting that includes some of the goodness from the S.M.A.R.T. model.

God-Inspired

> *"For I know the plans I have for you, declares the Lord, plans to prosper you and not to harm you, plans to give you hope and a future." Jeremiah 29:11*

> *"Delight yourself in the Lord, and he will give you the desires of your heart." Psalm 37:4*

God desires to work with you and to work powerfully on your behalf. As a Kingdom Driven Entrepreneur, partnering with Him to both create and pursue your goals is one of the greatest privileges you can ever have. How do you ensure that your goals are God-inspired and aligned with His purposes for your business? It's quite simple -- by seeking Him. Instead of dreaming your own dreams apart from God, consider dreaming with God. One of the best ways of doing this is to spend some time in prayer daily, inquiring the Holy Spirit, and listening for His voice. Some helpful questions to ask the Lord are:

- What is your heart concerning this business?

- What is your heart concerning those I am called to serve through my business?

- What is your heart concerning where I should be

focused right now?

Write down the ideas and the answers you receive. Write down all the questions you have. Talk to Abba, your heavenly Father, and place your thoughts before Him. You can also review any notes or journals that include some of the words God has spoken to you in the past. Quite often, there are treasures in those previously revealed words that can and should be included in your goal setting process.

Proverbs 16:3 says, "Commit your works to the Lord, and your thoughts will be established." Simply put, transfer the burdens of the work of setting goals to the Lord and trust Him with them. When you do that, your thoughts (intention, imagination, and plans) will be established (or fixed, ordained, and perfected) by God. You do not need to over-analyze or be fearful of whether the goals you've written down on your heart are in alignment with God's will. As you engage with the Holy Spirit, He leads and guides you into truth. Trust that as you are pliable in His hands and sensitive to His leading, God will place petitions, prayers, and desires on your heart. In addition to having the mind of Christ, you will be aligned with His will for your business, so you can move forward boldly in faith, making adjustments as needed along the way.

I should also caution you about something that may happen when you have God-inspired goals for your business. From years of experience, I can tell you that when you seek His heart concerning you and your business, you may find yourself writing down goals for things you never thought you wanted and never intended to do. When this happens, trust God and write it down anyway. It is an invitation to His best, an invitation to uncover and unlock prophetic destiny. Trust me; you'll never regret saying yes to it!

Limitless

Instead of focusing on what's "achievable and realistic" based on our current resources or circumstances, be willing to set goals based on what God is speaking to your heart. He is the Source - everything and everyone else is a resource. If He said it, you can believe it. Far too often, we make the mistake of putting God in a box, which is the last place He belongs in our life and businesses. After all, God is God! He is unlimited. He surpasses greatness. There is no one else in heaven or on earth that can do or even come close to the mighty deeds that He does! In Isaiah 55:9, the Lord declares that His ways are higher than our ways and His thoughts are higher than our thoughts. I am not talking about setting limitless goals out of myopic presumptions or self-serving ambitions, but rather leaning into the Kingdom reality that all the resources in heaven are available to you as you step out and faithfully do the things that God has called you to do in your business.

When it comes to goal setting, here's a basic rule of thumb: if you can easily think of how you can achieve all of the goals you set for yourself, it's just not big enough. However, when you can look at your list of goals that you created from seeking God's heart and say "Wow. I have no idea how this is going to happen. Only with You, Lord!" you're playing right into God's specialty.

Aligned

In addition to wanting to align goals with your core values and ensure that they contribute toward your broader business goals, you also want to ensure alignment with God's way of being and doing (in other words, with God's Word and His character). You also want to ensure alignment with the vision God has placed on your heart. Too often, the tendency to compare yourself to others leads to creating goals that are not authentic to you and how you show up in the marketplace. In such situations, some helpful questions to ask can include:

- What is my motivation for this?
- Does this support the bigger picture of what I am doing?
- Is there peace in my heart concerning this?

Transformational

As a Kingdom Driven Entrepreneur, you are an agent of transformation. You have been given the gift of a platform called business where you can bring glory to God, reveal His glory to others, and have both earthly and eternal impact through your work in the marketplace. By operating in excellence, you will have others see the Spirit of God working in you. You can stand for righteousness, express love extravagantly through your service to customers, and be a much-needed catalyst for enduring change.

When it comes to structuring your goals, keep transformation on your mind. What is it that God has called you to do? How are you going to serve as a transformation agent with *your specific product or service?* With some businesses, it may not be your specific products and services that will be transformational; instead, it may be something you do with regard to customer service, or perhaps something you choose to do with a percentage of the profits you receive from selling your products and services. Don't believe the lie that you have to have 7-figure profits in order to make an impact and have transformational goals. You don't. You can make an impact regardless of the size of your business, so don't despise these small beginnings because the Lord rejoices to see the work begin (Zechariah 4:10, NLT).

Transformational goals can be monetary or non-monetary. To have a better idea of what a transformational goal can look like and entail, consider these real-life examples of how other marketplace leaders have chosen to serve as transformation agents through their businesses:

- Using a percentage of profits to invest in homes that provide low cost housing for the homeless or the elderly
- Giving 10% of business profits to support your local ministry/church home
- Giving $1 from every sale to a non-profit that provides educational opportunities to youth
- Including a Biblical scripture on each paper cup served to customers (perhaps they have a goal for sharing hope and the word of God with a specific number of customers)
- Offering select scholarships for participation in your program or event
- Starting a corporate giving challenge among your employees by giving them $500 in cash, requiring them to give it away to people or donate to causes where they are afforded the opportunity to feel the impact or build a relationship (and have the employees share the stories!)
- Offering prayer and encouragement on a weekly

basis to employees and customers

Borrowing from the S.M.A.R.T. framework, a Kingdom driven approach to goal setting would also include **Specific**, **Measurable**, and **Time-Related**.

- You want to be clear and concise enough with your goals, so that anybody who looked at it could understand it quickly.
- Allow the goal to stand on its own without including detailed (presumed) plans of action.
- Use concrete criteria that can be tracked and measured to determine progress - even if you have a certain goal that is more qualitative in nature (e.g. Improve my confidence in hearing God's voice in my business), you can still set a quantitative measure using a ranking scale (e.g. ranking your current confidence and your desired confidence level)
- Include a specific time frame for completion

Applying God's Grace, Discerning His Pace

When it comes to having specific, measurable, and time-related goals, you will want to take some important Kingdom keys into consideration so that you can continue to operate in the power of God's rest and grace, rather than taking on the burden of doing everything in your own limited strength.

> **Key #1:** *You have freedom to make goals (plan), but the success of those goals and plans lies in God's response to them.*

Proverbs 16:1 says "The preparations of the heart *belong* to man, But the answer of the tongue *is* from the LORD." For added clarity, here's that same verse in other translations: "Mortals make elaborate plans, but God has the last word (MSG)." and "Go ahead and make all the plans you want, but it's the Lord who will ultimately direct your steps (TPT)." Proverbs 19:21 says "Many are the plans in the mind of a man, but it is the purpose of the Lord that will stand." As I often say, make your goals and make your plans, but hold them loosely. After all, God is the God of your outcomes!

> **Key #2:** *It is with faith and patience (perseverance) that you see the promises of God unfold.*

Ensuring your goal is time-based is a good discipline given that it sets an expectation to come into agreement by faith. Apart from helping you to prioritize your work and create a plan of action, it also gives you a means of accountability (whether that be with someone else or just yourself). For many people, a lack of deadline leads to procrastination. Having a timeline serves as a reminder to be diligent in both faith and action.

With that said, you never want to turn a deadline into an idol. Doing so is a recipe for condemnation and disappointment when the goal is not achieved on the timeline created. Idolizing deadlines also ends up creating undue pressure to perform and "grind it out" in your own strength, rather than working diligently in God's rest and favor. Sure, do create your timelines, but hold on to these truths as you do:

"For God is not unjust so as to overlook your work and the love that you have shown for his name in serving the saints, as you still do. And we desire each one of you to show the same earnestness to have the full assurance of hope until the end, so that you may not be sluggish, but imitators of those who through faith and patience inherit the promises." Hebrews 6:10-12

"For you have need of endurance, so that when you have done the will of God you may receive what is promised." Hebrews 10:36

"To every thing there is a season, and a time to every purpose under the heaven" Ecclesiastes 3:1

"For still the vision awaits its appointed time; it hastens to the end—it will not lie. If it seems slow, wait for it; it will surely come; it will not delay." Habakkuk 2:3

The Power of 90-Day Focus

There are many approaches to goal setting, but I want to encourage you to use this Kingdom driven framework to specifically set your goals on a quarterly basis. When you're doing business in partnership with God, led and empowered by the Holy Spirit, you should expect pivots, course corrections, and increased clarity as you move. Setting goals in 90-day cycles helps create space for the resets or corrections that you will inevitably encounter, without adversely affecting your focus or diligence. Setting 90-day goals allows for less overwhelming shorter-term strategic planning which I will share more on shortly.

I'm not saying that you cannot or should not have longer term goals. Quite often, God gives you a vision of the future that goes far beyond your present state of business. Take note of what He reveals and what is on your heart. Maintain a journal of what you believe may be longer term ideas and visions. You definitely want to capture those, ponder them, and review them regularly. However, I highly recommend a powerfully focused 90-day cycle for your goal setting and strategic plan.

As you're prayerfully writing out your goals, consider that there may be two types of goals that are on your heart to document. **Outcome goals** will be focused on the specific desired end. For example, I will increase the number of consulting clients I serve by 50%

or I will serve 500 students in my virtual baking course. Perhaps it may not be connected to anything numerical in nature, such as, I will identify and hire a Chief Operating Officer for the company. Often with outcome goals, you can take some steps in diligence that will influence the outcome, but the fact remains that you cannot necessarily control the outcome. That's ok, because as already discussed before, God is the God of your outcomes. **Process goals** are based on your behavior or strategies that will help you propel toward your outcome goals. For example, I will dedicate 10 hours a week for writing, or I will have business meetings with God every weekday Monday through Friday.

Pray, Write, Sleep, Review, Revise

When you are goal setting with God, it will sometimes be a multi-stage process. You don't have to rush through it. Pray and invite God into the process. Write down what's on your heart. Leave it alone and come back to it after you've slept and look at it again with fresh eyes. Revise it as often as necessary. You may even want to review it with someone who serves as an accountability partner, mentor, or source of wise counsel in your life. If you're married, review it with your spouse. Having an outside perspective can be truly invigorating in that they can lead to clarifying questions or greater insights.

I will be completely honest and tell you that there was not much 90-day goal setting happening during the first several months of Kingdom Driven LLC. My co-Founder Antonina and I had no idea what God was up to and what we were doing. We were operating in faith off of one word He gave us, which is that Kingdom Driven Entrepreneur was "a community and a movement that starts with a book." Our initial goal was to simply write the book and then start the community. After we released the book and started the community, we didn't really have a full picture of the "why" and God's heart on what we were doing, so we simply prayed on a daily basis. When it came to planning and goal setting, we spent several months in the "Give us our daily bread" stage. The goal was simply to hear and follow God and take the next best action we knew to do as a demonstration of our faith. It took nearly three years before I was able to set 90-day goals and strategic plans.

Now, don't get me wrong. I am not sharing this because I recommend waiting three years into your business to set 90-day goals. Far from that. I am sharing this because I want to release freedom for those who God is taking on a journey of "simply walk with me daily and I'll show you" right now. There is nothing wrong with that journey. It's a beautiful one of deep intimacy with the Lord, but it's also amazing (and a sign of growth in identity and Kingdom authority) to be able to set 90-

day goals with God, have a vision that goes far beyond your today, and work diligently in partnership with Him to witness a manifestation of what is on your heart come to pass.

3
FAITH IN ACTION

> *"So also, faith by itself, if it does not have works, is dead."* James 2:7

It's not enough to have Kingdom Driven goals for your business. It's a powerful start, but what happens after you've written them down? As a Kingdom Driven Entrepreneur, how do you take your goals and move forward towards achieving what God has called you to do in your business? You're probably thinking "I have to take action and get to work!" You're correct, but there's a lot more to be done. Remember that you completely tossed *achievable and realistic* goals to the wind. You've now replaced them with God-inspired, limitless, aligned, and transformational goals. When you're bold enough to do that, you better believe that you're going to have to do more than simply take action and get down to work. Here are the three steps that help you to move forward to achieve your Kingdom Driven goals:

1. Know that you can trust in God
2. Pray without ceasing
3. Take bold action

These steps are intentionally listed in a specific order because you can't truly engage your faith without knowing that you can trust God. Equally, you can't continuously take bold action on Kingdom Driven goals and achieve them without having a spirit of expectancy that only comes through faith. However, the reality is that you should do all of these steps simultaneously and consistently.

Know That You Can Trust in God

You mean *everything* to God. No matter what you may think or how you may feel, He is not mad at you! In fact, He's mad ABOUT you! He loves you so much -- with a love that is truly indescribable and unending. Nothing can separate you from His love! In fact, His love for you is the reason why you can trust Him. You can trust Him completely with your business. Meditate on the truth of these scripture verses:

> "Look with wonder at the depth of the Father's marvelous love that he has lavished on us! He has called us and made us his very own beloved children." 1 John 3:1, TPT

> "There is no fear in love, but perfect love casts out fear. For fear has to do with punishment, and whoever fears has not been perfected in love." 1 John 4:18

> "The Lord your God is in your midst, a mighty one who will save; he will rejoice over you with gladness; he will quiet you by his love; he will exult over you with loud singing." Zephaniah 3:17

Every morning, I thank Abba for loving me with a love that knows no bounds - it's everlasting. It's because I have a revelation of that love that I know that I can trust Him completely with my entire life, including my business. That isn't lip service either. I used to be a control freak before I prioritized cultivating an authentic relationship with Him. I have since been redeemed from my controlling nature, something I am much grateful to God for! I believe it's impossible to truly trust God if you don't make it a priority to cultivate an authentic relationship with Him. It is by cultivating your relationship that you will be able to have personal encounters with Him. He will show you more of who He is, and more of who you are in Him. You will experience God in ways you never experienced before or even thought was possible. As it says in James 4:8 (TPT), as you move your heart closer and closer to God, He comes even closer to you.

Trust in God is essential because without it, you will give up prematurely or fail to take action on directions you've received because they seem ludicrous. You may even reject a God-given goal or vision because you think you are unworthy or unqualified (which is nothing but a lack of trust in who God says you are and a lack of trust of what is possible with and through Him). You have to be able to move forward confidently, magnifying Him despite any circumstances that come your way, and be able to say "Lord, I trust You. I don't know exactly what I'm doing, but I trust that You are ordering my steps here."

Pray Without Ceasing

Being in business is not easy. When things aren't moving fast enough, it's tough to persevere on your own. When things are moving really well, it's tough not to get complacent. When you fail, it's tough to be confident, put yourself out there, and take a risk again. It is really tough to do all of it on your own, which is why engaging your faith is so pivotal to achieving all God desires for you in the marketplace.

Spiritual warfare is real. There is an enemy to come against you to distract you, place obstacles along your way, and make you feel defeated. You can also be an enemy to yourself due to the battle in your own mind and emotions! It's so important to pray and strategically intercede for yourself and your business. It is through diligence and prayer that the manifestation of all our goals will come through.

I believe that when Paul challenged believers to pray without ceasing, he was encouraging us to be consistent in prayer, persistent in prayer, and to maintain a spirit of prayer (an abiding presence with the Lord and dependence on Him). Here's a strategy you can put into place that will not only engage your faith (by hearing and declaring the Word of God), but also serve as intercession for your business. I recommend writing out a prayer that you will pray daily. It will be a part of your daily business meeting with God. The prayer comprises three main parts:

- Prayer of Thanksgiving
- Prayer of Confession
- Proclamations of Faith

Seek the heart of the Father and create your own prayer, including each of these three parts and the goals that you have written with God. While you will create your own prayer, I will share some examples in order to help you get an idea of what this may look like.

Prayer of Thanksgiving

In this prayer, you simply thank God for who He is in general, and who He is in your life in particular. Psalm 100:4 says "Enter his gates with thanksgiving, and his courts with praise! Give thanks to him; bless his name!" There is no better way to create an atmosphere of prayer than to thank Him because He is always so worthy of our praise! Here are some of the things I often say as my prayer of thanksgiving:

- Father, thank You for who You are. You surpass greatness and there is absolutely none like You.
- Thank You for your love that knows no bounds.
- Thank You for your amazing grace that enables me to do all that I am called to do and be all You have called me to be.
- Thank You for putting the will inside of me to hunger and thirst for your righteousness daily.
- Thank You for giving me even greater revelation of who you are as Provider; the Funder and Resourcer of my dreams.
- Thank You for your promises toward me and my family.
- Thank You for setting my mind on what the Holy

Spirit wants to do today

- Thank You, Holy Spirit, for always leading and guiding me into all truth.

Prayer of Confession

Romans 10:17 says, "So faith comes from hearing, and hearing through the word of Christ." It's important that you continue to hear the word of God coming from your own mouth. It is part of renewing your mind, aligning your heart with the Father's heart, and aligning your thoughts with the mind of Jesus Christ. Identify the scripture verses that connect with where you are right now and what you're believing for and write them down for the purpose of daily confession. For example:

- No weapon formed against me shall ever prosper (Isaiah 54:17)
- You open doors for me supernaturally that no man can shut, and close doors for me that no man can open (Isaiah 22:22, Revelations 3:7-8)
- You work everything out for my good and for Your glory (Romans 8:28)
- I recognize that with God, all things are possible (Matthew 29:16)
- I have eyes to see and ears to hear all that You desire for me to do in my business (Proverbs 20:12)
- I hear my Father's voice, and the voice of a

stranger I will not follow (John 10:5)

- My light shines before all men; they may see my good works and godly lifestyle and glorify You, my heavenly Father (Matthew 5:16)

You may even want to include statements of affirmation or statements of service rooted in scripture. Examples include:

- I do not worry, I do not doubt, I do not take no for an answer. If you promised it, I know You will do it and nothing will be able to come against me or that promise.
- I will not give up, cave in, or quit.
- I overcome every obstacle, I outlast every challenge, and I come through every difficulty better off than I was before.
- I thank you in advance for divine acceleration with [name of business] - that what would normally take a year, will take a month; what would normally take a month, will take a week; what would normally take a week, will take one day; and what would normally take one day, will be done in a moment.
- I have a spirit of excellence in every area and am fervent and diligent in my work.
- There is no shortage in You; therefore, there is no shortage in me.
- I magnify You over all circumstances.

- Let [name of business] be a reflection of You and Your greatness. Every person that comes in contact with [name of business] in any way will feel Your presence, Your peace, Your anointing, and Your spirit.
- I operate and work in truth, integrity, and love for others.
- I will be a blessing to all those who call upon me.

Proclamations of Faith

You end your prayer through a proclamation (or decree) of faith based on the specific goals that you have written down. In John 15:7-8, Jesus Christ promised, "If you abide in me, and my words abide in you, ask whatever you wish, and it will be done for you. By this my Father is glorified, that you bear much fruit and so prove to be my disciples." That is an astounding promise, yet he said it. Because he said it, he meant it. He also said (in John 16:24), "Until now you have asked nothing in my name. Ask, and you will receive, that your joy may be full." You know what Jesus also said? In Matthew 7:7-11, He said "Ask, and it will be given to you; seek, and you will find; knock, and it will be opened to you. For everyone who asks receives, and the one who seeks finds, and to the one who knocks it will be opened. Or which one of you, if his son asks him for bread, will give him a stone? Or if he asks for a fish, will give him a serpent? If you then, who are evil, know how to give good gifts to your children, how much more will your Father who is in heaven give good things to those who ask him!" That is why it is so important to abide, ask, seek, and knock with expectation as a Kingdom Driven Entrepreneur.

I make my proclamations of faith using the words "I ask and decree by faith that" and then follow up with the particular goal. This is where you take out the goals you have written out with the Kingdom goal setting framework - those goals that are now God-inspired, limitless, aligned, transformational, specific, measurable, and time based. For example, let's say one of your outcome goals is to serve 500 students in your virtual baking course over the next quarter. In that case, you can make your declaration of faith by saying: "I ask and decree by faith that I will serve with excellence 500 students through my baking course this quarter." After all the proclamations of faith are done, I seal the prayer by asking these things in the name of Jesus as he has instructed: "I ask and decree by faith all of these things in the mighty name of Jesus Christ, amen!"

Pray Daily

This powerful and strategic prayer is prayed with intentionality specifically concerning your business daily (and of course you can apply this to your overall life as well). I am not recommending this as your only means of prayer, as much of prayer is spontaneously Holy Spirit-led. There is beauty in embracing intentional prayer that is both planned out in advance with the Holy Spirit as well as those that are "in the moment." I also want to encourage you to not read your prayer to yourself, but actually proclaim it aloud. Use your mouth! There is a sound in Heaven, there is life (and death) at the power of your tongue, and you are a creator made in the likeness of God who created the world with His words.

Write your prayer out in a journal, notebook, or have it in a document that is handy on your smartphone in order to access it at any time. Engage your faith through prayer daily because the more you speak those goals and God's Word in that prayer, the more Heaven will respond, and the more you will see a manifestation of God's best in your business.

Take Bold Action

Armed with the revelation that you can truly trust God and the tools to engage your faith through prayer, you will have a great foundation for taking bold action with the goals you've set forth in your business. Oftentimes when God gives you a vision, He shows you an outcome, but you are rarely shown the entire process that must happen in between. It is in the "in between" that your faith is increased and you learn to trust God more.

As you begin your operational business planning in support of your goals, there are four key questions you will want to ask yourself (and the Holy Spirit): What actions should be taken? Who is going to take these actions? When do these actions need to be done? What resources are needed?

You want to have clear action steps written down to help bring your business goals to fruition. To prevent yourself from being overwhelmed, consider breaking out your 90-day goals into monthly goal increments. This provides focus and priority to what needs to get done and when to get it done. Think of the 30/60/90 day goals as miniature strategic business plans.

Write down the things you can do in the next 30 days, 60 days, and 90 days that will move you closer to achieving each of the overall goals you've set. It does not need to be an exhaustive list, but it should definitely be an impactful one. After having done that, you can determine the tasks or activities that need to be completed each week. Develop a simple system that helps you keep track of how you're accomplishing your tasks. This could be something manual that you write on paper, keep in a document or spreadsheet, or use a planning tool. Find a system that is simple and works well with your style.

FREE RESOURCE: *To download a 30/60/90 day operational business planning template, visit https://kingdomdrivenentrepreneur.com/goalsetting*

As you're mapping out your 30/60/90 day goals and action plan, you will likely realize the need for additional resources. Those resources tend to fall into the following categories: financial resources, human resources (e.g. staffing, contractors, vendors, partners), technology resources, skill development resources (e.g. books, courses, training). While identifying these needed resources, you can include any steps you are aware of toward acquiring them within your operational plan. Sometimes, that simply implies investing in what you need. Other times, it is not that simple as there may be other constraints. This is a good time to remind you that you have *all the resources in Heaven* available to you as you step out and do the things that He has called you to do in your business. Do not feel confined by what you can or cannot see. Trust God, praise Him in advance, and seek Him for wisdom and strategy for accessing all the resources you require. He truly is your Source and Provider of all that you need in your business!

Know that you can trust God, pray without ceasing, and take bold action -- these are the three Kingdom keys to helping you achieve the goals for your business in partnership with God. Remember that they don't work in isolation - they work in harmony! This is why it's imperative to do them all concurrently.

4

THE BOTTOM LINE

God has so much in store for you and your business that will bring glory to Him, serve your loved ones, and have eternal impact. This is why it's so important that your goal setting is not done by worldly standards. As a Kingdom Driven Entrepreneur, make sure that your goals are formed on the foundation of God's word and the leading of the Holy Spirit.

The Kingdom Driven approach to goal setting may be unpopular, but it's an approach that will bring God's best to you and those whose lives are impacted through the work that you do in the marketplace. It's a unique approach in that it is not done primarily in your own strength, but rather by the infinite power of God's grace. It's an approach that accesses Heaven's wisdom, economy, and unlimited supply.

It requires that you trust in God and believe that He

is exactly who He says He is and that you are exactly who He says you are in Him. It requires engaging your faith and maintaining an attitude of gratitude and praise at all times, while exercising your God-given authority through prayer and declaration of His word. It takes being bold in taking action as a demonstration of your faith.

God is all seeing, all knowing, and all powerful! Because of who He is, I encourage you to dream big with God. Don't box Him in. He's an awesome, uncontainable, and limitless God, so your goals should reflect that. As you delight in Him, He gives you the desires of your heart, so your goals should align with what He has inspired. He is the loving God that brings transformation when you're abiding in His presence, so your goals should be transformative.

Keeping these things in your heart along with the other Kingdom Driven goal setting essentials shared in this book will help you operate and steward a true Kingdom business that represents and reflects the heart of Abba and King Jesus. Remember to enjoy the process in the midst of it all. Enjoy the adventure of it all. When you do, you will experience God's best in business; the Ephesians 3:20 kind of best that is immeasurably more than you could ask, think, or even imagine.

ABOUT THE AUTHOR

Shae Bynes is a passionate storyteller, bridge builder, and strategist who ignites and equips leaders to be catalysts for transformation in their spheres of influence.

Known as "Chief Fire Igniter", she has reached over a half million aspiring and current entrepreneurs around the globe through her devotionals, books, courses, short films, and podcasts. Her teaching and mentoring provide inspiration and practical strategies for doing business in partnership with God for greater Kingdom impact in the marketplace.

Shae co-founded the Kingdom Driven Entrepreneur movement in 2012 and her most popular book *Grace Over Grind: How Grace Will Take Your Business Where Grinding Can't* is shifting the manner in which people live, work, and engage the world around them.

Shae Bynes

Whether she is sharing on platforms publicly or consulting privately, you can expect Shae to deliver an abundance of truth with love, grace, and contagious joy.

Shae holds a bachelor's degree in Computer Science and Masters of Business Administration from the University of South Florida and University of Florida respectively.

Shae is married to her husband Phil and is mom to three beautiful daughters, ranging from toddler to college student. She has a healthy addiction to sunshine and water and calls the Fort Lauderdale, Florida area her home.

ABOUT KINGDOM DRIVEN ENTREPRENEUR

The Kingdom Driven Entrepreneur is driven by the mission to inspire, teach, and mentor entrepreneurs who desire to be led by God in their business, so they can experience His best and have a greater Kingdom impact in the marketplace.

Our vision is to see individuals, families, cities, and industries radically transformed for God's glory. We envision a community of thriving entrepreneurs with businesses that serve as a sign and wonder to the world; replete with the unconditional grace and boundless power of Jesus Christ.

It's a globally thriving movement and we invite you to join us:

KingdomDrivenEntrepreneur.com

BOOK PREVIEW

INTRODUCTION

"Too many believers in business idolize hard work. They exalt hard work over the presence of God in business."

These are the words that Holy Spirit shared with me one day as I was at the beach, enjoying the sight of my girls laughing together as we waited for our family photographer to arrive. Two simple statements from my favorite Teacher, packed with profound and convicting truth.

In the world of entrepreneurship, *hustle and grind* is a celebrated way of life. Some of the expressions you'll commonly hear or read on t-shirts, mugs, and social media memes are "I'm on my grind", "Rise and grind!" ,"Team No Sleep", "I'll sleep when I'm dead", "I hustle hard", "Good things come to those who grind"...

The list goes on.

You may even use some of these expressions yourself presently or perhaps you did in the past. There's no condemnation or judgment here. I used to run a website with a tagline that included the phrase "get your hustle on."

Needless to say, I get it.

Well-meaning Christians have modified the idea of hustle and grind to make it more Jesus- friendly which has led to phrases such as:

- Pray. Grind. Repeat.
- Wake. Pray. Grind.
- Eat. Pray. Hustle.
- Hustle for Jesus.
- God. Goals. Grind.
- Grinding for God.
- Push. Pray. Grind.

The phrases are different, and they sound more spiritual, but the prevailing mindset is the same.

When you look up the definition of grind in the dictionary, it is defined as *requiring much exertion* and *excessive hard work*. Synonyms for grind include the words struggle, attempt, and strain. When you look up the definition of hustle, it is defined as *making strenuous efforts to obtain especially money or business*. This should not be your testimony, and quite frankly, it doesn't have to be.

You may be thinking to yourself "Come on Shae, these are just words... it's just an expression!" But the cost of a hustle and grind mindset (even if you pray first or say you're doing it for Jesus) is simply too great for Kingdom-driven entrepreneurs. There is a supernatural realm that many Christian business owners are failing to tap into because they are busy grinding; running fast and furious to accomplish as much as possible, as quickly as possible.

This is not God's best, and if your heart is to see the realities of the Kingdom in your business, your industry, your city or even the nations, it's imperative that you create and maintain a lifestyle of working by God's grace rather than by your grind.

Consider the words on the following pages to be an invitation from Abba, your heavenly Father, the Ultimate CEO, and best business partner you will ever have.

It's an invitation to live and work by the grace that He has so lovingly provided for you to experience His best in your business. Notice that I didn't say your best, but rather *His* best. I'm talking about the Ephesians 3:20 kind of best; which is immeasurably more than all you can ask or imagine according to His power that is at work within you.

My prayer is that this book will either serve as confirmation of what God has already placed on your heart, while helping you to grow on the path you're already on, or that it will provide you with new revelation; igniting faith and action for a different lifestyle of doing business.

Let's begin!

GRACE OVER GRIND IS AVAILABLE FOR PURCHASE IN PAPERBACK, HARDCOVER, KINDLE, AND AUDIOBOOK!

GET YOUR COPY AT
HTTP://GRACEOVERGRIND.COM

Made in the USA
Monee, IL
17 March 2021